PRAISE FOR THE AUTHOR

Virg is a successful businessman with refined wisdom and interpersonal skills. Through the years I have learned to know Virg, he has shared several different experiences from his life story. I have learned that his success has been a journey that included difficult and trying times, as well as successful endeavors through perseverance. The wisdom he has acquired is just as valuable as any physical asset. I admire his steadfast faith and how important his daily walk with Jesus is, no matter the circumstances. Virg and his wife, Von, have become two of my dearest friends. They have been there for me and my family as we have celebrated exciting events, and upheld us in prayer and loving support as we walked through one of the darkest and most difficult storms we have ever experienced.

BETTY BROCKMUELLER, REGISTERED NURSE

Virg is the same person whether it has been 10 minutes since you've talked to him or if it's been 10 years. He makes me feel like talking to me is exactly what he wants to be doing at that moment. He is genuine and honest. He cares for people who are in his life like they are all his family. He has a gift of inclusion like no other.

BETH COX, FORMER ASSISTANT

Virg has played such an influential role for me, as he is a mentor in my professional, personal, and spiritual life. Virg leads by example, he displays what true integrity and selflessness is to all those he comes in contact with. He invests himself in others as he serves, listens, and prays for them. Over the years, I have come to Virg with many questions, and he has always been very open and gracious with his time, wisdom, intelligence, and humor. Virg has the ability to help you realize and achieve your true potential in all aspects of life. He will be the first one to congratulate you when you succeed and the first to help you back up if you fall short. Virg truly embodies what genuine leadership is, and generously shares that gift with so many people in his life.

JACE VANDER MATEN, JUNIOR ADVISOR AT TALL GRASS WEALTH MANAGEMENT

"Virg has always been a constant in our very dynamic family. Cindy trusted him, the kids trusted him and he was one of the few people that I knew that his word or his handshake was worth more than any signed document. I trusted Virg with our finances, but more importantly, I trusted him with our spiritual and personal lives. All three of our children and their spouses have a special relationship with him and know that he cares about them and has their best interests at heart. Virg has truly impacted our entire family."

DR. JAY BOBB, PARTNER AT PIPESTONE SYSTEMS

My relationship with Virg has been with him as a listener, encourager, mentor, friend and someone who could speak words of wisdom when I could not think rationally. We all need someone in our life that can help us process life during the good times and the hard times.

Virg has experienced losses and successes, but the losses have not been life defining, but instead lessons in character-building and fuel for the next leg of his journey.

Because of his spiritual walk with God, Virg was able to walk with me while raising my family, building a business and during the cancer journey of my wife.

Virg's transparent approach to life allows him to walk in your shoes to see a bigger picture of where the journey of your life could take you.

VIRG CHRISTOFFELS, FOUNDER OF CHRISTOFFELS HAIR RESTORATION AND ENTREPRENEUR

In times of change, we need leaders in our lives to guide, direct and challenge us. Virg is one of those leaders in my life. His wisdom is timely, practical and effective. He has a way of delivering the right word at the right time that makes a major difference.

JEREMY BROWN, BEST SELLING AUTHOR AND CEO OF THRONE PUBLISHING GROUP AND STORYWAY

The day I met Virg I knew I was in the presence of a leader and a person that truly cared about you as a person. I am in the financial services industry because of this man. My personal life, my business skills, and how I lead my teams have all been enriched by what Virg passed along to me during the 10 years I worked alongside him. I serve others and strive to live with a deeper purpose thanks to Virg and all that he taught me during our time together. Virg was like a second Dad to me and I will be forever grateful that he came into my life at a young age and time when direction and life skills and development were so needed.

CHRIS COX, ENTREPRENEUR, OWNER OF CORNERSTONE WEALTH MANAGEMENT IN ARIZONA

When I met Virg in early 2000, I had no idea the long term impact he would have in my life and the relationship that God would create between Virg and our family. We met through a mutual friend when our family was looking for help in preparing for our financial future. Virg was different from other financial advisors we had met in the past. Through Virg's actions it was evident that he was interested in more than just a business transaction. He wanted to build a long standing relationship. From birthday cards, to Christmas greetings, Virg stayed in touch with us outside of his role as our financial advisor and we knew we were more than just a "client" to Virg. Over the years, Virg became a mentor, encourager and advisor in our lives. Virg's integrity and

Virg has been a difference maker in both my personal and professional life. If I had to pinpoint one reason why, it would be that he authentically cares. In a world full of surface-level interactions, it is refreshing to connect with someone who listens to understand and doesn't just listen to respond. Two minutes into a conversation with Virg, you feel like you have been friends for life. Well, little do you know, you actually did just make a friend for life. He is loyal, faithful, prayerful and is in your corner cheering you on, backing you up, encouraging you and challenging you through both the good times and the bad. Virg has been gifted amazing wisdom through all of his personal and professional experiences and I (along with many others) are so blessed by the freedom with which he shares! There have been many times where I struggle to articulate what exactly I am feeling and he has an amazing ability to identify it and offer the right words at the exact right time. I am humbled and grateful to call him a mentor and a friend for life and am blessed to have had a front row seat as his business successor to witness the true impact he has had on so many people.

NICK AAMLID, WEALTH ADVISOR, PINNACLE WEALTH, VIRG'S BUSINESS SUCCESSOR

I had the privilege of working at DeJongh Financial as Virg's executive assistant, albeit for a relatively short time. I'm not sure I have ever worked for or alongside a person who demonstrates integrity and Christian character as Virg DeJongh. Prior to working for Virg, our paths crossed at church and school events where he would support his grandchildren. While my employment for Virg brought us together on a daily basis for a few short years, our friendship has continued ever since.

As an entrepreneur, I have observed Virg integrate his life calling's of work and faith in all areas of his business dealings and life coaching. His sincerity humility, honesty and generosity are very evident whether you are doing business or having a cup of coffee with him.

As a family man, I have observed his strong love for his wife, Von, his three children, and all of his beautiful grandchildren. Whether it's out on the lake with his family, or attending his grandchildren's ball games or programs, his genuine love for their faith and wellbeing is of greatest importance to him.

As a man of God, I have observed Virg's fear of the Lord, love for others and faith integration. His commitment to daily devotion time is inspiring. The value he places on relationships based on honesty, integrity and loyalty prove that he cares more about people than any business or financial successes.

JILL HAAN, FORMER EXECUTIVE ASSISTANT

character were emphasized by his faith in God and it was evident that God was the director of Virg's life, both personally and professionally. He never shied away from working in our lives. Virg has influenced us over the years with his guidance and encouragement. Our family is truly blessed from knowing Virg.

KANDY BAUDER, CLIENT, WRITER

Virg was a specialist in the industry recruiting, mentoring and coaching new associates in the financial industry with a variety of backgrounds. His personal and business experiences coming from a farm business work ethic and high expectations carried with Virg into a very different culture. At age 38, Virg was one of the most coachable persons I knew. He was in the very front of people going through changes in their life. Virg's team was responsible for helping highly successful entrepreneurs in the financial arena, in careers that ended being a new, exciting and fruitful life.

Virg and Von have been great role models for their family, friends and business associates through their marriage, their leadership, integrity and character. They have created a wonderful legacy for their family. Virg desires and has a passion to have a meaningful impact with others. I have known Virg over 30 years and this is his DNA. May God bless this new venture and impact many.

DOUG BECK, FRIEND/CEO OF FIVE STAR FINANCIAL SERVICES

ON THE VIRG

VIRGIL DEJONGH

ON THE VIRG

HOW TO MOVE FORWARD THROUGH LIFE'S BIGGEST
QUESTIONS, CHALLENGES, AND OPPORTUNITIES

DEJONGH
PUBLISHING & CONSULTING

Throne Publishing Group
1601 East 69th St N Suite 306
Sioux Falls, SD 57108
ThronePG.com

DEDICATION

To my special lady, the mother of our three awesome children - Troy, Tami, and Tricia - and loving Nana of our sixteen beautiful grandchildren.

She never loses sight of what's real in life. Von has experienced less than a predictable, "normal" life. Von has never questioned our wins and losses, is unwavering in her love for me, and never questioned our journey. Von is content wherever God directs us. We prayerfully made life decisions hand in hand. We share our conviction that we are not our own. All we have is from the gracious hand of God. Von and I are of one heart and one mind in our faith and love for Jesus Christ, our Savior and Lord. Though shaken at times, our trust in God is rock solid!

I can honestly say in fifty-three joy filled years of marriage, I have never seen my life partner angry. I say this out of amazement and deep respect.

Most importantly is her tender heart, character and patience. The Lord in His divine wisdom knew I needed a gentle and patient wife!

My ultimate treasure is my precious wife and her quiet force as the Christian mother to our children! Von is my first and last stop. She is my cheerleader through this exciting journey together. She is my best friend, my constant love and God's greatest gift to me!

Von, you encouraged me to write, and I thank you for embracing me in this new adventure!

I dedicate "ON THE VIRG" to you, Von! I love you!

To God be the Glory!

TABLE OF CONTENTS

INTRODUCTION

Walk with the wise and become wise;
associate with fools and get in trouble.
Psalm 13:20 (NLT)

There is a very old saying that declares that no man is an island. On the surface it is easy to dismiss that statement as referring to the importance of having friends, or being around others. But I have come to believe it is much bigger than that. I have come to see that *who* we are around is more important than the number of people who are around us.

Have you ever noticed how we often begin talking like the people we are around? Many times, we do not just adopt their word choices. Sometimes we start picking up their habits, too. The problem is, there is a tendency to adopt their not-so-good behaviors.

It is human nature to conform to the people we are around. The people we choose to hang around with in life define who we become. We tend to mimic or mirror other people's behavior, and that can lead us down roads we never intended to go.

The good news is that if we are around people who inspire, challenge, and mentor us to move in positive ways, we usually adopt those behaviors as well.

That means it matters who we surround ourselves with. I have met many people in my life whose choices were impacted by the people they were around – whether good or bad. We have a choice in who we allow to speak into our lives, and that may be one of the most important choices you make.

Throughout my career, I have had the privilege of hearing many individual and family stories. I learned that we often share common struggles and worries. And I saw how the right word at the right time could make all the difference in the world.

That was certainly my own story.

My hope is that through my own experience, and the choices I made along the way, and the voices that spoke into my life, you will find inspiration and determination to make the changes you need in your own life. No matter where you have been, or where you are going, there is always opportunity to change. It may not be easy, and it may not always be fun, but when thoughtfully planned and executed, change can move you into a new identity.

Use this book and the study questions included in each chapter to help guide you as you learn how to Think Well, Live Well, and Finish Well™.

CHAPTER 1

WHEN THE CROPS FAIL

SOMETIMES YOU JUST KNOW

Growing up, farming was all I knew. My father was a farmer, so in my young mind, living and working on the farm was the only, and best way to live.

Farm life was very different back then, and we certainly did not live like many do today. Life was very simple. In fact, my family did not even have a TV. Our lives centered around dairy farming and hard work.

Dad was driven and I looked up to him. So my way of getting recognition was to do what he did, which was work hard.

Like most children, my dad's acknowledgement was extremely important to me. I needed it, and I learned early on the way to get it was through working hard and exceeding what was expected of me. So that is what I did.

Back then, many parents did not make a point of telling their children they were proud of them. But although he never said it, I knew Dad was pleased with the way I worked. So, I made a point of doing more than my fair share, and often did things beyond what he expected.

I remember working alongside him at a very early age, as he did chores. When I started helping, I was so young, he had to buy special pails that I could stand on and carry milk in the barn. I remember standing on a step stool to pour milk into the larger bulk tank.

The work we did was physically challenging. There was a lot of hay to bale since we had dairy cows. Often, my father would hire young men from town to help with the work. Baling hay was labor intensive, and even grown men would sometimes have difficulty keeping up. Still, although I was just a squirt, I could throw bales of hay better than most of them.

A typical day on the farm began about 4:30 a.m. and most of the time you worked hard until bedtime. You did what you had to do to get the job done, respected authority, and that meant doing some things you did not like or want to do. But none of that mattered to me. I knew I wanted to be a farmer, so I accepted the challenges that came with it.

Even as a very young child, I knew I wanted to do more than the average farmer. I wanted to be the type of farmer that people looked up to.

Growing up, I went to public school for the first eight years, then to Christian school from ninth grade on. Changing schools was a big change, but we did not think much about it. We were expected to adjust, and that is what we did.

After graduating, most kids I knew went on to college. But I knew I was going to farm the rest of my life, and knew college was not for me. I had the rest of my life planned out.

WHEN EVERYTHING CHANGES

Then, in 1965, life changed dramatically. Tragically, my mother took her own life during my senior year of high school. We never knew why, but she left five children – four of which were still at home. The youngest child was only eleven years old when she died.

Mothers are the glue that holds families together. Losing her to suicide was not only heartbreaking, it was confusing, and changed our family. It was hard on each of her children, but my dad was never the same afterwards. Still, we pressed on and did what we had to do.

One year later, almost to the day of her death, I went to war. I grew up during that time. That was when life became real. War was serious business for an eighteen-year-old. The military taught me that life was sometimes non-negotiable. It reinforced the belief that there are times you have no choice but to keep pushing forward.

During my time in the military, I spent two tours overseas. It was a new experience in a lot of ways. But that is where praying became central to my life. I looked forward to hitting the pillow and having time to talk to God. During that time, my relationship with the Lord grew deeper and more personal than ever before.

My time in military brought happy times too. I married my high school sweetheart, Von, while I was still serving in the Navy. While we courted, I had her sold on the benefits of being a farmer's wife, so it was no surprise when I started farming right out of the military.

I was excited to begin working with my dad again, and I was still very determined to be the best farmer I could be.

Before I had enlisted in the military, my dad and I had agreed that I would come home and farm with him. However, while I was serving overseas, my dad remarried, and it changed the dynamics on the farm. His new wife had younger children, so his focus was no longer on farming together.

During that first year of farming with him, I began to realize I was more of a hired hand than a potential co-owner of the farm. I was very disappointed, and I knew I could not work that way, so I had a heart-to-heart with my dad. He really wanted to move away from the house he lived in on the farm, because that is where my mom had taken her life. That was when I got a loan and bought the farm where I grew up and my dad moved on to another, smaller farm.

BIG CHANGES AHEAD

The first year of farming on my own went fairly smoothly – at least as smoothly as farming can go. I still had a dream of excelling as a farmer. I knew deep down that I would not be satisfied being average. We had a lot of livestock and a lot of land. I was always growing, and had a desire to expand further.

Still, I remember standing in the shop when the

local banker called to ask me if I wanted to buy more land. Financially I could have supported it, and it was a good opportunity. But, something in me did not feel right about it, so I turned it down. Looking back, it was the right decision.

Then, in the late 1970s and early 1980s, out of the blue, interest rates went sky high. Many farmers we knew had leveraged a lot, and ended up in very deep trouble. Several farmers we knew lost everything. People began to panic.

We had invested in a lot of cattle, and that hurt us in a big way because we still had expenses such as feed and veterinary bills to pay. Like any business, farming has operating costs such as fuel, feed, fertilizer, and machinery. Now, we were paying twenty percent interest for those things, where we used to pay seven to eight percent on operating loans.

During that time, Von and I had many conversations about what our worst-case scenario would be. We tried to figure out whether or not we should get out of farming. For a while, we thought it would turn around. Many bankers believed the crisis would peak and the economy, and farming would eventually go back to where it previously had been. That seemed to make sense, but over the next few years, we watched it steadily decline, until eventually, everything seemed to be upside down.

The uncertainty of what my future held hit me hard. Once you are a farmer, there is a mindset that you can never do anything different. We had made good progress since I had begun farming, and things had been going well. Eventually though, things got serious enough, and we had to face the fact that changes were needed.

That realization was devastating. As a Christian, I had always felt called to farming, and it was where I found gratification, so I could not make sense of what was happening.

In farming, your home is in the middle of your business, so you never get away from it. Going to bed can seem like an escape, but when you wake up everything is still there. When things started going south, it felt like I was going to a funeral every day.

I got quiet, because in my mind, there was nothing we could do about what was happening. Von could see I was shut down, and she cried a lot of tears over it. We were struggling.

Back then, Von and I would listen to Dr. Charles Stanley on the radio every day. It seemed like everything he spoke about related to the uncertainty of our situation. His words went deep and spoke into my heart.

Around that time, Von started getting severe headaches and was hospitalized in an effort to figure out what was going on. When the doctor said nothing was physically wrong, we were almost disappointed because it felt like we were facing another unknown. One of the many doctors who saw Von asked me what my occupation was. When we told him, he said a lot of his patients were farmers, and that I might want to consider a career change. His words hit me hard, because I did not like that option. Still, it was clear the stress of our situation was seriously affecting Von.

Even our children struggled. At one of their school conferences, the teacher pointed out the changes she had seen in them over the previous year. When we shared what she had said with a close friend, he told us that when parents do not tell children what is going on, they often assume their own version of the situation. He suggested we let the kids know what was going on, so we did. But even though we were able to help them understand, it was disheartening to see how it had affected them.

Throughout married life, Von and I had a routine where every night we would hold hands and pray together. We continued to do that during this time, which was important to us. However, during this season, our prayer time usually started with me praying and Von crying.

My prayer was always some version of, "Lord, show me how to save this farm." We knew prayer was the answer, but we were not getting any direction, and the answer to that prayer seemed as empty as a big blank wall.

Eventually I got frustrated enough to shift how I prayed. When I finally changed the way I prayed and asked, "What do you want me to do, Lord?" things changed.

THE SHIFT

It is a lot easier to get *into* farming than it is to get *out* of it. I still needed to look at all my options, so I took my farm records to a third-party banker, and asked him to review my operation. It took about two or three weeks for him to go through everything, but eventually he called and asked to meet us.

The memory of that day is still very clear. The appointment was at 9:00 in the morning, and we drove on icy roads to get to his office. I remember him sitting back behind his big desk and saying. "You know Virg, I went through your records inch by inch. You're a good operator. Your marketing is good."

He told me that he was willing to finance me for another year of farming, and that he could loan us the money necessary to put the crops in. The news did not sound too bad, until he said, "But…"

The banker explained that if we had an average year, with an average crop, and had no losses, we would be able to pay the interest only on that loan. It meant we would have all the effort and all the risk, but would be no further ahead and have made no gains.

I heard myself say, "Shut the books, I'm done."

That was it. After years of farming, we were done. We did not say much after that. Von and I walked out, went to the bakery to get coffee, and we were still mostly quiet as we drove home. Then, somewhere on the drive home, she tearfully asked me what I was going to do. It was a fair question. I was unsure what my next step would be, but I did know for certain what I was *not* going to do. I knew I was not going to give my soul to the farm.

Many times, people need to know what their next step is before they move on. It was not like that for me. I knew something had to shift. And to me, it was very clear what I was *not* going to do.

There was a lot of chaos in farming at that time.

Some people chose to stay in and fight, but eventually went down with the ship. A lot of people who had watched my business over the years were shocked at my decision to leave. Many of them thought I should have hung on. They believed I should have been able to make it work.

Even family did not understand. My dad said I was giving up too quickly – which pained me. My brother was affected in a big way because we had helped each other farming. He was very understanding, but got quiet when I told him. But I had made my decision, and I was at peace with it.

My exit strategy was simple. I did not want to let everyone know until I got all my commitments paid. It was the right thing to do, but not always the way things are done. I remember many of the bankers I had worked with were surprised that I proactively left farming.

I was not going to farm, but I had to do something. So, soon after the farm sale, I began working as a farm manager. The man I worked for was capitalizing on the farms that were going under. It was a large operation, so he needed a manager. I took the job reluctantly, because I needed to work. My job was to help make it grow, but it was much more stressful work. Some days I felt like I was in the pick-up twenty-four hours a day. I planned on leaving after the first year, but he paid me more so I would not quit. So I stayed one more year, which meant putting in many, many stressful hours of work.

I knew I should probably leave, but did not. When I blacked out at home from sheer exhaustion, Von said, "enough," so I gave my notice and resigned that spring.

After that, I interviewed with several different businesses, but nothing felt right to me. Around that time a friend said, "Virg, there's life after farming." He was probably right, but I was not sure how that would look for me. All I had ever known was farming.

That friend was in insurance sales, and recommended I look into that work. I had avoided sales my whole life, but I started talking to a few companies. I still was unsure if insurance was the right fit for me. It felt like a dead end. Von and I kept praying and I kept looking. Then one day, a friend rode past my place on his bike and asked me how I was doing. During that conversation, he referred me to his friend Bob, who was from Willmar, Minnesota. I promised I would make one more call.

When I connected with Bob, he said he would like to visit with me *and* my wife the next day. That seemed strange to me. Von had not been with me on any other interview, so I told him I did not think she needed to be involved.

Then Bob said something very interesting. He told me, "You are going through a lot, and your wife is too. You need to be together on this." He also said if she did not come, there was no sense in us meeting. So, Von came along to the interview.

Bob was a few years older than I was. Like me, he was raised on a farm, and had a high school education. He told us he had always wanted to be in this business. Before this meeting, I had spoken to a lot of people, and attended a lot of "meetings" that ended up being mostly booze and big talk. That was not a draw for me, but this conversation was different.

Bob showed leadership by insisting that Von must be there. I was intrigued. As we began, he asked me to tell him my story. I shared all our ups and downs. I explained that I needed income because it was a critical time for Von and me.

He leaned forward and said "Virg, you have so much to give."

Those words blew me away. It was really big for me. Up to that point in my life, I could not see that in myself. He continued, telling me that many people need to hear what I had to say. The way he spoke to me was so radical! No one had ever said things like that to me before. His words were powerful and gave me a glimpse of hope and renewed confidence.

Bob told his own story of being on the farm, going into the military, and then going into business. As he shared his life story, he did not flaunt the successes he had experienced; he just unfolded a picture for us. It was a whole new experience for both me and Von. We could relate to him in a lot of ways.

When we asked him what he actually did, he brought out a paper, a pen and showed what he did when he met with clients. At the end, he asked "Could you do this?" I agreed that I could. Then I asked him if he thought I could make at least thirty thousand dollars my first year, and more importantly could he *guarantee* it.

That is when Bob said yes. He would guarantee what I had asked, if I did two things:

1. Learn the presentation.
    and...
2. Work hard.

I understood what working hard meant in the context of farming, but I wanted to know what it meant in this business. Bob explained that it meant sitting down with ten people each week, and giving the presentation he had just given. That was it.

He said if I committed to doing it this way and stayed teachable, I would be successful. And if I did what he said, he would take responsibility for the money.

What Bob had done did not seem like a presentation; it was a conversation. I liked Bob, and what he offered. The process was simple and straightforward, not all glitz and glamour. I knew right then I was in, and made a promise to him on the spot.

Von and I left that meeting very hopeful for the future. We both believed meeting Bob was the answer to the many prayers we had said together.

QUESTIONS

Often, we stay too long in situations because we have difficulty letting go, or feel there is nothing else we are qualified to do. Reflect on where you are stuck and what holds you captive as you answer the following questions:

What is it you have held on to far longer than you should have?

1

What is the
cost of hanging
on to a
situation too
long?

2

What are two reasons you are having difficulty leaving the situation you identified? Be specific as you think through the reasons you stay.

3

When were there times you have prayed that God would fix a difficult situation according to what you believe is a solution, rather than asking Him what His resolution is?

4

Virg and Von

Virg and Larry at harvest time.
Circa 1981

*Virg preparing the soil for planting.
Circa 1981*

CHAPTER 2

A CHANGE OF SEASON

"If you're ever going to do stupid,
promise to call me first."
Virg DeJongh

THE OPPORTUNITY

In order to sell life insurance, I had to be licensed. It is a complicated and intense process, and the whole thing was foreign ground for me. In order to study enough to pass the required test, I had to go to Minneapolis to take classes. I stayed at Northwestern College because it was cheap. It worked, but if I am honest, I felt pretty low. I had been a successful farmer, and now I was reduced to staying in a college dorm to save money.

One night while I was there, Von called and told me a friend had been in an accident. He and two other guys were in a car/truck accident. They had hit another car with a mom and her two kids, and everyone had died. I was shaken. This guy had been bigger than me in farming, and I had been a bit jealous of his success. Now, none of what he had accomplished mattered because he was gone.

It was a come-to-Jesus moment. I had been feeling sorry for myself. Here I was at the age of thirty-eight, having to stay at the college, and trying to pass this test. It seemed unfair, but that friend's accident made me see it differently.

I realized the journey I was on was not just because something had happened to me. Right then I saw that leaving farming, meeting Bob, and changing careers was a God-orchestrated opportunity.

QUALITY MENTORSHIP

I did not realize it at first, but working with Bob was a profound experience, because it provided more than a new career – it opened a relationship with someone who would become a life-long mentor. Mentors are there to guide others to greater success. They are knowledgeable and trusted, and provide help and guidance. I had never experienced someone pouring into me like Bob did – not growing up, or through my years of farming. This was new territory, and the example he gave became an important part of how I lead today.

We all need someone who sees the best in us, and

who believes in our value. The right mentor is someone who buys into who we are, not just what we can do for them, and that is what Bob was for me.

The right mentor at the right time is a game changer, but you have to be prayerful and careful. Finding a mentor is almost like looking for a spouse. You cannot just buy in; you have to know who you are looking for.

If you are changing careers like I was, it is even more important to have the right mentor. You want to capitalize on what you have done with your life so far, but there is a potential to sell yourself short, and become connected to the wrong person. That can happen because you are looking for answers, but you are fragile and vulnerable. I can tell you, when you feel like you "just have to do something," it is a dangerous place to be.

By the time I met Bob, I had been through many circumstances that had not worked out well. I knew what it felt like to be in situations where I clearly did not fit anymore. You should spend time praying about the next step. Finding the right mentor takes prayer and thoughtfulness.

You know you have found the right person when you have a sense of comfort, peace, and answered prayer.

Both Von and I had been bathing our situation in prayer. After that first meeting, we both felt at peace – and that is key. That unified experience with Von was in part a confirmation of answered prayer. We both felt that we had God's affirmation, and the calm that came with it was a wonderful feeling. After that first meeting with Bob, we both knew the search was over.

In every mentor/mentee relationship, there must be an uncommon amount of trust on both sides. It is like turning over the steering wheel in a car you are driving to someone else. You better be able to trust them to keep you both out of the ditches, on the road, and going in the right direction.

I trusted and sold out to Bob in that first hour I spent with him. He told me he believed in me, and I gave my word that I would do what he told me to do. After that conversation, I felt hope for the first time in a long time.

You need to find someone who is willing to walk alongside you, and guide you. The one who is willing to say, "That's not the right place for you."

There are a lot of voices, and a lot of chaos out there. It can be confusing and distracting, so you have to make sure you are tuning in to the right voices. A mentor should be the right voice, and should be able to help you avoid the unnecessary chatter of wrong voices.

In difficult times, it is common to begin second-guessing yourself. Once you do, it does not take many other voices to weigh in and add to your doubt. Your best defense is to be selective about who you talk to. There are times you may need to politely walk away. Remember… Anyone throwing careless opinions around does not have regard for your welfare.

A good mentor is blatantly honest, and cares enough about you to point out things that could bring you harm. Mentors:

- Help us see where we need to grow and improve – even when we do not see it.
- Encourage our personal and professional growth. They care about the whole person.
- Inspire and help us to keep going. They raise our spirits, and offer hope.
- Genuinely care, and care for the right reasons.

But being a good mentee is also an important part of the equation. As a mentee, you play a part in the success of the relationship too. Mentor/mentee relationships require both parties to be open, honest, committed, dependable, and consistent. It is a promise that must be kept!

To get the most out of mentoring, you must be coachable and teachable. The minute you become unwilling to learn, you limit yourself and reduce the ability of your mentor to help you grow. In order to have a good working relationship, it takes a minimum of two people who are totally committed. If one lets go, it is over.

Bob was as serious as a heart attack! It was clear he kept his promises, so I believed I could trust him. He made sure I understood what it took, so I was prepared to face any challenges that might come up. Because of this, I respected the business I was entering into and the way Bob approached business and success.

When I first met Bob, he told me I had a lot to offer because of my experience. He could see what I had learned through farming and life in general, and he knew how to help me grow that experience into a meaningful career.

I was committed to do what I needed to make this new career a success. But Bob's mentorship played a significant role in my success.

My advice for anyone without a mentor is to keep searching until you find one. Bob did not just show up. I was desperate, and I spoke with a lot of people before I met him. I may not have consciously known what I was looking for, but I knew enough about life to know what did not work. When Bob asked me to tell him my story, and shared his, it brought us into each other's lives.

What are the
elements of a
good mentor/
mentee
relationship?
Describe them
in detail.

1

What are ways your life could change if you had the right mentor to support you? Take a moment and dream about the changes you want to see happen, and describe how a good mentor could help you achieve those goals.

2

Who is your mentor? If you do not have a mentor, name the one person in your circle who you might connect with. Describe how you might approach that person.

3

CHAPTER 3

THE RIGHT
HELP MATTERS

"You have to be around and listen to the right people, and to have discernment about the people you're listening to."
Virg DeJongh

THE POWER OF VOICES

Many times, change can cause us to become fragile.

After meeting Bob, Von and I were on a high. Our perspective had changed, because that meeting made us feel like things were coming together. We left that day feeling a sense of peace. And the two-hour drive home gave us a lot of time to reflect on all the reasons this was the right decision.

After we got home, I went to the local quick-stop gas station, and I ran into someone I knew. As we talked, he asked what I was up to so I excitedly told him what I was going to do. To which he replied, "You just made the biggest mistake of your life."

It was like being sucker punched. He told me his company commonly replaced a lot of the business of the company I had just agreed to work with. His advice was if I had not signed anything, to get out of it. Then he invited me to an upcoming meeting at his company.

His words left me confused and wondering if what I had done was the right thing. I began to second guess the promise I had made. I had been so sure that the decision to work with Bob was the right one. Was my promise to Bob a mistake?

When I got home, and told Von, she suggested I call my friend Dave. He is a youth pastor and good friend. We had prayed together, and met many times before, and I trusted him. I took her suggestion and gave him a call.

As I unfolded all that had happened, Dave just listened patiently. I told him I had not signed anything, but I *had* given my word. When I was done talking, Dave pointed out that Von and I had been praying about what my next step should be before I met with Bob. He reminded me that I felt peace when I had given my word to him. And, most importantly, he reminded me that I had given Bob my word.

Dave's words brought me back to where I had been when I left Bob's office, and I knew then what I had to do.

Right then I realized I had fallen into the devil's trap, and I could not believe I had fallen for it! But I was not there for long. I made a decision to honor my promise to Bob; I was not going to go back on my word! My word was my bond!

The thing we have to realize is that we have an enemy who does not want us to succeed. Satan has an army out there waiting to devour us, and he works best when he can get us to doubt what God is doing and what He says.

I almost let one guy take me down. I let his words sway me and get me to doubt what God had done. It was a lesson that showed me there are right and wrong voices. Later on, I learned that guy was not such a good person. He had a lot to say, but nothing to back it up. He was a man with a big hat and no cattle.

You need to know that in moments when you are vulnerable, it is human nature to look for affirmation. You will naturally be drawn to the opinions around you to provide confirmation. But you also need to know that is when you are most vulnerable to both good and not-so-good voices.

I had finally found a fit in the opportunity Bob presented, so I was relieved and at peace. I had disarmed myself thinking the battle was over. I HAD taken off my armor and laid my weapon down. This was a great reminder that we cannot do that. Soldiers do not put their weapons away, even when the battle goes quiet. When we let down our guard, we are exposed, and the enemy can easily swoop in and attack.

In this circumstance, Von's recommendation helped me avoid making a wrong decision. I am so grateful for her suggestion to call my friend. She instinctively knew I needed someone else to weigh in. In moments of weakness, you need someone who is going to be blatantly honest, and your spouse cannot always be the only person.

The words that sideswiped me came from a guy I barely knew. But it is important to realize the negative voices in our lives do not always come from strangers or distant acquaintances. They can also come from close friends, and even family. That may seem shocking, but all of us are flawed in some way. We must understand that people may not have our best interest at heart. It is very rare that others will deeply care about what is going on in your life, so you must be cautious about whose voice you listen to.

It is important to recognize the difference between good and bad voices. To really figure out who

you should be listening to, notice their conversations. Do they constantly find fault or judge? Does
it feel like they always see the worst in any situation?
If you answered yes to these questions, you may
want to consider shutting out that voice, or at least
not taking the words they say to heart.

Like I said, we are all looking for affirmation. But
you have to know where to look for it. You are not
always going to get it from:

- Media
- Friends
- Family
- Acquaintances

We cannot live life alone, or put our lives on cruise
control, mindlessly going about our business. We
need to be purposeful. We must have people around
us to help us grow, learn, and excel. But we cannot
allow just anyone to speak into our lives. The right
people are going to be willing to walk alongside us,
and partner in the rough places as well as the good.

THE POWER OF PRAYER

When faced with making decisions, prayer is pivotal. God's voice is the first one we should turn to. Sadly though, we usually only go there when we have run out of other options.

When the farm crisis happened, Von and I put ourselves on pause and asked the Lord for direction. We poured our guts out to Him in prayer! He is the *only* One who understands it all, and that is because He knows us, inside and out. Really... why would I not go to the One who knows it all? God is the ONLY place you will get the real answers. There is no one that *loves* you more, *cares* for you more, or *wants* you to be fulfilled more than the Lord.

However, even when we do pray, the challenge many of us have is waiting for the answer. Waiting may seem unproductive, but it is valuable time. That is when we are shaped and prepared for the next step. It is where we learn to trust God in deeper ways. And, it is where God reveals our weaknesses. What we need is to be patient, but keep trusting God.

Looking back, I wasted a lot of time asking God to tell me how to fix the farm. That question was really asking Him to resolve the problem in a way that made sense to me. Asking what He wanted me to do changed the question to one that gave room for His direction. And that is exactly where we needed to be so that God could reveal His plan. God knows much better than we do what our next step should be. I could have asked the Lord much earlier what He wanted, but because I am human, it did not happen until I was at the point of exhaustion. I had to be totally spent before I turned to Him. The lesson here is that we do not have to do it that way. It is a choice.

Going through all those struggles taught me something. It showed me how God orchestrates our paths, and puts the right people around us. It was a great example of how He sets the table. It was a big deal then, and even now I am awed by the impact it had on Von and me.

Von and I took turns praying. We did not have an agenda; we just knew that God was our source. We did not pray fancy or elaborate prayers; we just poured our hearts out to Him.

Those times of prayer and pressing in strengthened our relationship with Him. Looking back at that time, it is so clear how God used that time to grow us – even though we did not see it then. Many times, that is how it is. We do not see God's hand in a situation until we look back at it.

This scripture really talks about the need to wait for Him:

> *Psalm 46:10*
> *Be still, and know that I am God!*
> *I will be honored by every nation.*
> *I will be honored throughout the world.*

As soon as we begin to quiet ourselves, and recognize He is God, our situation becomes clearer. It is not always an easy thing to do. We often think we need to say or do something, but sometimes you have to just sit there and wait. Remember, we are the ones who are broken. We are the ones looking for direction, and He is the one who has the answers we need. Most importantly, we must remember, and believe that Jesus has our best interest at heart.

LOCK INTO THE RIGHT VOICES

Listening to the right things is critical. There are practical things you can do to make sure the voices you lock into are the right ones.

When you begin to doubt a decision you make, reflect on when you had peace about it.

Ask yourself why you made the commitment in

the first place. Many times, it is important to repeatedly reinforce that moment. I went back to the meeting Von and I had with Bob over and over. I had to remind myself it was God ordained. Then when the voices come in, go back to the moment where you had peace in the situation. Von and I knew we had prayed, and had peace when we made the decision, and our confidence came from knowing that.

Fight the negative voices by remembering what God has done.

Give yourself a pep-talk. Early on you need to remind yourself that you can do what you need to do. Truly, every day you have to remind yourself why you are in business. Reaffirm what you already know by going back to why you are doing what you are doing. Ask yourself what you went through to get to where you are.

And *never* let your ears hear your mouth say, "I'm just trying this."

The things we say out loud are easier to believe. By telling yourself you are "just trying" something, you are saying there is a plan B. As humans, there is a tendency to give up earlier if we allow ourselves an out.

One of the most important things you must do is to have a close friend or mentor who will speak truth and ask the hard questions like my friend Dave did. I would say it is really a requirement. It is great if you have a spouse to talk to, but you cannot just rely on him or her. Your spouse is in the situation with you, and may not have the perspective you need.

It is vital to have someone who understands what you are battling. Mentors will not tell you what you want to hear; they will tell you what you *need* to hear. They can help you remember what you are doing, and why.

The most important thing you can do is to be brave and remember that God is with you and He will get you where you need to go. Just like it says in one of my favorite Bible verses:

Joshua 1:9
Have I not commanded you? Be strong and courageous! Do not be afraid or discouraged. For the Lord your God is with you wherever you go.

Where have
you let the
wrong voices
speak into your
life, or into a
specific
situation?

1

What are ways you can block out, or eliminate wrong voices?

2

How has prayer
changed the
way you make
decisions? If
you have not
been praying
through
decisions, how
would your
situation
change if you
did?

3

Who are one or two people you would consider the "right voices" in your life? If you do not have at least one person, commit now to identifying him or her.

4

CHAPTER 4

GOOD SOIL

"When you don't keep your word, you may think you're letting everyone else down, but you're truly letting yourself down."
Virg DeJongh

YOUR WORD IS GOLD

The conversation I had with that guy outside of the gas station seemed innocent enough, but what he said made me question the promise I had made to Bob. Those words could have influenced me to back out. In the end, though, I knew I had given Bob my word, and to me, that was as serious as a signed contract.

My word is important to me. I always want to be known as someone whose word is gold, and you should too. A promise that is kept is like good soil. When the soil is good, what grows is healthy. When we make a promise or commitment, we should do whatever possible to keep it.

Promise keepers keep or follow through with their commitments or intentions. You will recognize them because they are truthful, trustworthy, and re-liable people. If you watch people long enough, you can usually tell if they keep their word.

Bob and I both believed that giving our word mattered, so the commitment between us worked. It is a matter of honor to me to do what I say I am going to do. Even in that very first conversation with Bob, I knew it was to him too. In all hones-ty, keeping our word should be important to every one of us. If you commit to something, you follow through. Period!

The way we keep commitments tells the world a lot about our character, and our word has everything to do with who we are.

When people do what they say they are going to do, it shows they are honorable and honest. If we do not follow through, we lose integrity and are not seen as someone with character. It stands to reason that lying should not be tolerated. If you catch someone blatantly lying, how do you *ever* know when you are getting the truth?

Do not give your word if it is not something you can keep. There are a lot of promises out there that, by design are never meant to be kept. You see it in our society, in the media and in advertising. They are meant to draw you in and grab your attention.

These promises are used as illustrations only. But those types of promises often leave a bad taste in our mouths. We do not trust them, and they are great examples of the importance of doing what we promise.

COMMITMENT

Back when I was young, a lot of business was done on a handshake. But things are different now. Business is conducted differently, and contracts are needed, and include a lot of small print, because sadly, people's words cannot be trusted.

I understand that it is important to be careful when relying on someone's word as a commitment – especially when it represents a contract. If you are going to hold someone to a promise, then it must be someone whose word you trust. In my case, I believed I could trust Bob's word, because I could see his commitment was as good as mine. Still, whether a contract is signed, or a promise is given, you should always have the commitment to keep your part of it.

My advice is that you do not sign a contract, or make a commitment unless you are sure you can keep your word to yourself first. You are the only one who knows if you are telling the truth, and if you will follow through with the promises you make. Know what you are capable of doing – or not doing. Then, when you make the commitment, stick to it.

This scripture says it all:

> *Psalm 89:34*
> *No, I will not break my covenant;*
> *I will not take back a single word I said.*

You cannot control whether or not others keep their commitments; you can only control what you do or do not do. Your word should matter most to you. You want to be seen by your family, your friends, your mentor, and your associates as a promise keeper.

Let your word be gold.

When have
you been
impacted by
someone who
did not keep
their promise?
What lessons
did you learn
from that
experience?

1

Are you known
as someone
who keeps their
promises? Why
or why not?

2

How can you
know if
someone is a
promise
keeper?

3

CHAPTER 5

TIME TO SOW

"Don't overshoot the runway. Get away from overly high expectations and face reality."
Virg DeJongh

STARTING IS KEY

The way we prepare or begin sets the tone for everything that comes later on. It is the foundation. Knowing that, we should do what we need to do to prepare. We should set realistic goals that push us higher. We must avoid setting overly high expectations for the outcome. Sometimes setting unrealistic goals does more to harm us than help.

How we start matters because it determines our success or failure. If we do not do things right from the start, we will *never* do them right. Getting off track at the beginning sets a pattern. It goes back to commitment. We must commit to how we are going to move forward and stick with it right from the start.

Once you know what your plan of action is, you

cannot give yourself permission to be reckless, and do less than what you set out to do. When I started, I committed to Bob that I was going to make ten face-to-face interviews a week. Now, when I made that promise, I did not know what the results would be, so there was nothing to keep me on track with that *except* my promise. For me, doing anything less than what I had promised was not going to work, so that is what I did.

It is also important that you do not start with an exit-strategy in place. All other options have to be off the table. Never say "I'll see how this works." Or, "If it doesn't work out, I'll do such-and-such." When you give yourself a way out, you sabotage your success. It is human nature to look for the exit when things get difficult. I have seen so many people fail because when they faced challenges it was too easy to walk away. Do not give yourself that option. There is no plan B!

Going deep during your searching process is critical. Do not take the first thing that seems like it will work. Do your homework, and make sure you understand what you are getting into. The more you know, the fewer surprises you will have down the road – at least as far as the business is concerned.

Remember to pray about it before you start, and

while you are looking. Von and I felt peace about my commitment to Bob because we had spent a lot of time in prayer before and during my search. And, when you pray, be willing to listen for God's leading. Do not just ask him to give you the answer *you* want. Then, before you decide to make any commitment, ask yourself these questions:

- Can I do what I am committing to do, and do it always?
- Will I allow myself slack, or do this to the best of my ability?
- What am I going to do if there are surprises, unexpected changes, or difficulties?
- How will I feel if I do not fulfill the promise I am making?

When you do make a commitment, go in knowing that you have done your homework, researched your options, and prayed about it.

THE IMPORTANCE OF FOUNDATION

Have a talk with yourself about expectations. This is key! Ask yourself if you are going to be someone who others want to imitate. For me, it was important to make a difference through whatever work I did.

Set realistic boundaries, and keep them. I had

promised Bob that I was going to visit ten people a week, so I had to do that. Right from the start, I intentionally made the decision to get the weekly quota in by Thursday so I would be sure to get it done. I made the commitment, and I followed through.

Have a good and realistic plan. I knew working with Bob was where I was supposed to be. I also understood that, just like in farming, I was going to do what I had to do to get the job done. So, my plan was to approach this new career like I had farming – with everything in me.

Do more than what is expected. When I was in the military, I often worked twelve hours a day. I did my job, and sometimes the jobs of others, not because it was required – because that was the work ethic I had developed working on the farm. There were those who said "Virg, we'll all get out the same day, your extra work isn't going to get you out any faster." But it did not matter, because I have always believed you give more than the bare minimum.

Start right. I did not want to prove what I could do to Bob as much as I wanted to show myself. When you start out with that attitude, you are demonstrating your commitment to yourself, your spouse, your family, and your mentor. In everything, do what it takes.

Here is why I say the first week sets the tone. If you are not intentional about what you do those first days, the next week will be easier to do a little less, and every week after will be a little less. Your commitment is a foundation for your success. It is like setting the forms for cement. Are you setting forms for a small house or a big house?

ASK THE QUESTION

At one point, I had a performance coach help with my business. It was during a time when I had brought many people into the business. We were growing, but things were so-so, and I just was not happy with the way things were going. The performance coach suggested that to move to the next level, I needed someone in the office to run the paperwork so I would be free to do business.

From my viewpoint, I did not see how that was possible. Plus, there was going to be a cost to add another employee. When I hesitated, he asked me, "How important is this to you?" Of course, my answer was that it was very important. I had paid for his opinion because I wanted to improve what we were doing. It made sense to take his advice. So, we hired an assistant, and in the end, it was one of our best decisions. Going forward, I often ask that same question of others who are faced with tough choices.

"How important is it to you?"

You see, sometimes you cannot see the forest for the trees. I trusted what the performance coach was saying. If I had not asked for his help, I might have stayed in the same situation for a long time. And if I had not answered that question the way I did, I am *sure* I would not have seen the benefit of changing. If what you want is important, and the solution is going to work, then why not do it?

This is vital! If something is not growing, it is probably dying. You never want to stay where you started. Ask, "What do you want this picture to look like?" Write down what is realistic, but then push yourself past that boundary. That is the attitude I had when I started. I figured if I was good at getting ten interviews a week, then why not do more?

Mindset is such a big deal. How we think shapes where we go. We have to guard our thoughts. Scripture tells us:

> *Guard your heart above all else,*
> *for it determines the course of your life.*
> *Proverbs 4:23*

When you farm, there is a lot of "think time" while you are getting the work done. It can be a good thing, but many farmers let their minds focus on the negative, difficult, or challenging parts of farming. And you do not have to be a farmer to get stuck in wrong thinking.

What we think defines everything we do. And it is important to understand that thinking is something we control. We either think in healthy, productive ways, or we engage in "stinkin thinkin." If you do not know what that is, let me explain. It is thinking that has the power to lead someone in unhealthy, unproductive, and unacceptable directions.

As soon as I got my license, Bob sent me out with his son alongside to help. I remember his son calling Bob to say we had a good day, and it surprised me. It did not always seem like we were having "good days." In *his* mind we were talking to people and having good conversations, and that was good. I had to learn that "good" is in the eye of the beholder. I could *choose* to see the good, or I could choose to see the bad.

It is important to guard our hearts and minds. When we do that, over time we will build up the confidence we need to follow through with what we say we are going to do.

How much confidence do you have in your own ability to do what you want to do? Answer that question out loud. It is great if others have confidence in you, but hearing that others have confidence in us will not be enough. Bob once told me, "You're going to want to find another you, but you can't - there's only one you." That was powerful, but it was not enough to keep me going every day. I needed to have confidence in myself. You not only need to have the confidence; you need to hear yourself say it out loud.

Still, we have to give ourselves grace. It takes time for your old self to learn to do new things. When we are doing something new, it is like flying an airplane for the first time. We may be skilled at driving a car, but now we are going to have to learn a whole new set of switches, gears, and rules.

When I started working in insurance, I went from coveralls to a suit and tie overnight. I called it culture shock! It was a new career, a new way of doing things. I had to adjust. When I started, my "office" was in my home. It would have been tempting to show up for work in my comfy hang-out clothes. But when I got up, I showered, dressed, and put my suit and tie on. It was a physical demonstration of how serious I was about the commitment I had made. I wanted my family to know I was working, and most importantly, I wanted *me* to know I was working.

What I did started me strong, kept me strong, and later on, helped me get others going strong.

YOUR COMMITMENT

Sadly, it is rare to see commitment in action. I learned early on that not everyone was as committed as I was. At one of my first group meetings, there were a lot of guys who had not followed through with their ten contacts. There were many reasons given, but for the most part, it came down to the fact that they just could not pick up that phone. They had made promises, but there was no follow-through – all thunder and no rain.

Do not get me wrong. The first six months were not easy. If you had asked me, I doubt I would have said I was having fun. But I was determined to focus more on the making ten contacts, and not on how I felt. It is okay to be realistic about your comfort level in those early weeks or months. Just know your feelings will pass. You are learning a whole new culture, and a whole new way of doing things. Do not expect it to be all fun out of the gate.

After about twelve months, I began to enjoy what I was doing. Still, even though it got easier, I did not let up on my commitment to have at least ten visits a week. In fact, I did not change that goal until I was much further on in my career, when I was at the point where I trained others. And even then, I made sure I had a goal. It may have shifted, but there was still a goal, and I still worked to meet it every day.

Be careful when a little success comes along, that you do not give up on your goals. Do not let yourself become lazy or complacent. When you become successful, focus on what it is going to take to keep you growing. You must remain persistent at every step in the journey. There are casualties in being casual!

How does the
way you start
out impact
your success?
Describe what
happens in
detail.

1

How is what
you are doing
(or going to do)
important to
you?

2

Where have
you let "stinkin
thinkin" creep
into your
thoughts?
What will you
do to change
that behavior?

3

What are two or three ways you will stay focused when things are not fun or easy?

4

CHAPTER 6

PLANTING SEED

"Always seek God's truth! Truth is truth — even if you don't believe."
Virg DeJongh

THINK LIKE A FARMER

As a farmer, the first thing I would do each day was look out the window to check the weather. God and nature were in control and set the stage for what was able to be done each day. I was in control of how I responded and responsible for doing what needed to be done. In that role, you do what you need to do, and when there are challenges, you face them head on. Still, your world is the farm and the weather.

When I worked with Bob, I was on my own. I had my own business, and the United States was my territory. There was a lot of freedom in that. All I had to do was talk to ten people a week. But there were challenges there too.

I quickly realized I could not just make ten appointments and expect that every one of them would stick. The only way to make sure I had ten appointments a week was to double-book. That way, if I got to the day and one cancelled, I still had the other. If both were still on the books the day of the appointment, I just moved one to the next week. I learned that if I set up fifteen appointments per week, I usually ended up actually meeting with ten.

My personal goal was to have all my appointments done by Thursday night. Friday was about getting paperwork completed, then we would enjoy a fun weekend. That was a big deal, because when I farmed, weekends were rarely, if ever, free.

One time, I got to Thursday and realized I would not have ten appointments for that week. So, rather than miss that week, I called my uncle and asked him if we could meet. He agreed, and when I showed him the presentation, I made a very big sale. He ended up buying life insurance for his wife, and later when she passed away, it allowed his family to continue on the path they were on.

Farming is a culture *and* lifestyle. The work ethic most farmers have is part of that culture and is based in a mindset that goes deep. You go into farming with everything you have and you give it the best you can. But in the end, what happens is up to God.

There are many parts of farming that are not

desirable. Sometimes livestock dies, hail comes, or crops fail. You have to face those things with a certain amount of resilience. You must have the will to keep doing what has to be done, and to make it work. You have to face the fact that sometimes things are going to seem impossible or at the very least, challenging.

I remember when my twin girls went to work one summer, at the local meat packing plant. Most of the time they hired these young people for the worst jobs. The first night my girls went to work, they were excited for the opportunity to have jobs and make some money. But after their shift, they were standing at our bedside weeping because the job was so hard. They wanted to quit, but I told them they had to stick it out for an entire week. If at the end of the week they felt the same, they could leave. By the end of the week they decided to stay. It was a valuable lesson on perseverance, and one they still talk about today. In fact, that experience has become the "tough talk" they use with their own children!

Sometimes you have to stay past the hard part.

Often when we run into difficulty in our work, we think it is time to leave. Farming had taught me that you work through the hard things. When I started in the insurance business, I did not always like what I had to do. I met people in all kinds of circumstances, and all kinds of weather, and many times at nine o'clock at night. Sometimes it was just hard.

Farming had taught me to keep going even when it was difficult. Farmers do not know what the day will bring, but no matter what, they have to persevere.

We have to mentally prepare for what will come. Know that there will be good times and hard times, but commit to sticking it out to the end. It is not a good idea to start a business believing it is going to be a bed of roses. If you do, as soon as it gets bad, you have a reason to bail.

Know yourself well, and know how you are going to react when it gets rough. And, it helps to have others around who can help you move past the disappointments.

One night I came home and three people cancelled. It had already been a rough week. I called Bob, and he said, "Tomorrow's a different day." It helped me shake it off and move forward. I knew he was right. I could have chosen to disregard his words. But if I had given myself a way out, I may have given up. Having your mind made up makes a big difference.

FINISHING

The qualities of a good finisher are quite similar to those of good farmers.

Farmers make hay while the sun shines. That means you do something while you can because the situation may not last. When there is a lot of business, that is great! But do not sit back and rest because business is good. In business, you have to be able to pivot and move onto the next thing. When three people cancel, you go on to book three more. Farmers often face tough decisions. For example, if hail hits your crops and you lose a significant part of the crop, or are wiped out completely, you have a decision to make. Will you decide to replant, or take what you can get from the crop? Those are tough decisions, and often you have to make them quickly because you are against the clock. That will happen in business too. When faced with hard choices, use what you know to make the best possible decision. Then, leave it up to the Lord.

Farmers have the work ethic and the mindset of taking it to the finish line. They know there are good seasons and bad, and they usually have no control over which it will be. In the insurance business I had some control, but not always. I still had to work with the end in mind.

Farmers use what they know about the seasons and conditions to plan. You cannot let emotions dictate your strategy or decisions. Go for what has the best odds. Again, there may be many voices, telling you what to do. But in the end, it is up to you.

Farmers do not look at their work based on how many hours they put in a day. There is an expectation of the work, not the hours. Many times, farmers work around the clock to get to the finish, and harvest before the snow or frost comes. It is a mindset of "Do what it takes."

Know this, there is more than one way to view fulfillment. Ranchers see things differently than farmers. Some of them still have an old west mentality and measure satisfaction as pastures filled with cattle. But to me, gratification is looking out on a nice-looking field. It is a fulfillment that is found in the work of your hands. It is the same in any business. Be grateful for what you are able to do, and be thankful for the blessing of a good outcome.

HARVESTING

Finishing and harvesting go together because you cannot do one without the other, and you must prepare for both. In both finishing and harvesting, how you end up is, in part, the result of the work you put in.

In finishing and harvesting, you look at what it cost you to do business in retrospect, and begin making plans for next year. It is a time to reconcile. In farming, those plans are often made before the next year begins, and sometimes you have to approach business the same way.

In the end, it is never about what you are going to do, it is about what you DID do. Decide what success looks like, and then determine what you need to do to get there. It is not just about the steps you need to take. You must ask yourself how much you are willing to do to get there. And if you are married, include your spouse in those decisions. In order for it to work, you must both be on the same page. You both need to be honest and transparent about your expectations.

It is about establishing the path you are going to take once you go forward. And once you step onto that path there is no looking back. You cannot let those bad days – and there are going to be bad days – trip you up or move you off the path. Adjust as challenges come, but keep moving forward. Remember, do not allow yourself to have an option to quit.

The good news is that when you move through the difficulties, it gives you confidence in yourself, and it gives others confidence in you.

In my new business, I always figured, "It's me, the phone, and the car. The only one who can screw this up is me." I wanted to be successful, so I knew I had to do what was necessary.

Your plan should fit the business you are in. I planned to meet with ten clients a week, and here is the formula I used:

50	15	10	5	50
You have to have **fifty** good referrals to be successful and feed future business.	Out of fifty good referrals, you can expect to have **fifteen** actual appointments.	from those fifteen appointments, you will have **ten** actual interviews.	From those ten interviews, you will have **five** sales.	From those ten interviews, you should have **fifty** (or more) new referrals.

Every number in this plan matters. Each one relies on the one before it. But, even if you are successful with the numbers, you have to be consistent. You cannot rest once you hit your mark. Doing this consistently is what fueled my fast growth. Over the years I saw many people drop out when they got to the five sales, but you have to get referrals. Without them you have no future business. I always asked for referrals. If *your* business is fueled by referrals, you must always ask too.

You have to know the numbers that work for your business, and then DO the numbers. Whatever that looks like for you, the key is to be consistent.

Still no matter what you do, there will be times things do not go as you hoped. In sales, rejection is a given. When I met with clients, I always told them no matter what decision they made, we were going to have a good conversation. That mindset changed how it felt when clients said, "no." By doing that, I made sure rejection or disappointment did not stop me.

Rejections sometimes cause us to lose confidence. But when our confidence is up, we do not succumb to fear of rejection. You have got to come into this with the right perspective. I always say that a "1099 person" is focused on building their net worth, but a "W2 person's" worth is measured by the size of their paycheck. They are both different worlds, different mentalities and different life experiences. I'm not saying one is better than the other, but it is important for you to make this distinction because it will establish how you think every day.

How have the undesirable things in your position caused you to lose focus on the end? What can you do to move through those times?

1

What does
success look
like for you?
Describe it in
detail.

2

What are two
or three steps
you can take
to get to the
success you
described in
question
number two?
Be as detailed
as possible.

3

How do you plan to approach rejection? Write down one or two strategies you can use.

4

CHAPTER 7

HARVEST BLESSINGS

*"Everyone has authority in their lives —
whether they acknowledge it or not."*
Virg DeJongh

THE PHILOSOPHY

Everyone has a philosophy in life – whether they are conscious of it or not. A personal philosophy is simply a set of guiding principles that we live by. Usually our philosophy influences what we say, how we live, and how we interact with others.

My personal philosophy is this: **Think well. Live well. Finish well**™.

THINK WELL

My philosophy starts with the way we think. I believe everything we do hinges on thinking well. Our thought life is always revealed in our lives. How we think, what we think, and even how *often* we think are going to come out in how we live.

Many people do not realize that thinking can be controlled. We must be intentional with our thoughts. They must be nurtured, guarded, trained, and have to be respected. This is a very BIG deal because this shapes the path we follow, and how we respond to life in dramatic ways.

Thought life is where our character is exposed – especially during difficult or challenging times. Ever see someone who usually comes across as calm and collected lose it when they get stuck in traffic? That person may have trouble in their thought life.

Character is made up of our heart, mind, and soul. It is the seed of our lives. If you want a good harvest, you have to plant good seeds.

To think well, you have to be deliberate about how and why you think things. Sometimes, we think a certain way because of what we learned at home, or from friends or peers. Other times, we let "stinkin thinkin" set up, and grow in our thought lives. It is not always easy, but we must know what is at the source of our thoughts. Getting to the source helps us figure out how to change thoughts that are holding us back or hurting us.

I have found the best way to impact our thoughts is to read scripture. You should be in God's Word until it sinks in, and your life reflects it. God's Word is like good seed for your thoughts. Still, it is not something that just happens, and you cannot get it by just showing up to church on Sundays. It has to be planned and purposeful. If the soil and seed of your thought life are good, you are going to see a good harvest.

Thinking well takes time, and is a lifelong process that takes effort. *Thinking well* sets the course for our lives.

LIVE WELL

When I say "Live well." I am talking about living the life God intended for you.

It starts by honoring God in everything you do. It is about doing what is right, not just what is convenient. Still, that does not mean there are never mess ups, mistakes, or challenges. Living well comes through setting a course that is based on obedience to God, not on what everyone else is doing. If you do that, no matter what you go through, at the end of your life you will have lived well.

I believe a well lived life is available for everyone. Like our thought life, it takes intention, and daily work. Living well is not a once and done thing. There have to be checkpoints such as accountability.

It requires us to be humble and teachable. Just like it says in Micah 6:8:

We must walk humbly before God.

We should not let the events that happen around us change how we live. Still, when our lives are in transition, living well can look shaky. When we are in transition, it is usually a time of testing. Like an athlete, our strength and endurance are tested. But if we press in and do what we need to do, we can survive it. When we are able to do that, we often end up stronger than we were before, and in a better place. What is most important in transition is to trust God. Know that He does not change, and He will be faithful to the end.

FINISH WELL

I believe that at their core, everyone wants to finish well. What sets us apart is how we define it.

Many people spend their lives believing that it is about money or fame. Some people think it is about how much they own. There are probably as many ways to define finishing well as there are people. But I define it as finishing the race God has set before us.

It is not only about success, or what we typically think of winning. It is about doing what you were created to do. It means making the most of what we are given, and never giving in to the temptation to settle for less than we are capable of.

Finishing well is not necessarily about money or success. It is about the relationships you have and the life you live. When my friend's wife died, they had six years to deal with the rollercoaster experience cancer usually brings. When the time came for her to go into hospice, she told him she was ready. While she was there, they spent time together, but did not need to hash out, or say things that had been left unsaid. They had already said it all, and they were at peace with life and with God. *That* is finishing well.

Living a life with intention for the purpose God designed for us is what it is about. We were created to be in relationship with Him, to serve Him, to honor Him, and to share His love with others. A good life is the by-product of living a life that honors God.

Matthew 25:21
His master replied, 'Well done, good and faithful servant! You have been faithful with a few

things; I will put you in charge of many things. Come and share your master's happiness!'

Living a good life can start at any time. If you have not lived with the resolve to finish well, I recommend you start today.

To sum it up, thinking is the seed that God gives us to live our lives. Living well is what we do with it. And finishing well is in our own earthly harvest and gives glory to God. The best news is that all of it, **Thinking Well, Living Well, and Finishing Well**™ is the call for all of our lives.

How has your
thinking
revealed
good and
not-so-good
character in
your life?

1

What is the
source of some
of your own
negative or
non-productive
thoughts?

2

How are you
honoring God
in everything
you do? If you
are not, how
can you change
that?

3

What are one
or two ways
you can
intentionally
live?

4

How does your life reflect the purpose God designed for you? If it does not, why?

5

Describe what finishing well looks like for you. How will you make sure you continue to move towards that goal?

6

CONCLUSION

There is so much that impacts our lives. Family, friends, peers, experiences, jobs, school, and the media can play a role in how we live. But the good news is, it only feeds into our lives if we let it. There is great opportunity to learn from others, and to teach others what we have learned. What we learn through our life experiences can and often does help others by giving them the opportunity to learn from past mistakes, triumphs, revelations, and lessons learned.

There have been so many experiences and people who have played a role in who Von and I are today. There were many people who spoke into my life, and encouraged and pushed me along the way. This book is just a glimpse into the relevant and deepest lessons my wife, Von, and I have learned throughout our lives. There is so much we discovered along the way about ourselves, our God, and people. We learned the right and wrong voices to listen to. And we found out a lot about ourselves in the process.

As humans, we are created for community. We often learn more socially than we do in traditional settings, and many times those are the lessons that stick best. My hope is that you can use our life lessons to better understand the importance of thinking, living, and finishing well.

In the end, though, it is up to you to take hold of the lessons. No one can force you to do anything.

You play the biggest role in what you think about, how you live, and how you finish. But having the right people around you can greatly improve your chances of success. Mentors are a valuable gift you give yourself. Choose people who have your best interest at heart, and remember that you must always remain teachable.

Most of all, remember that none of this is possible without God. He is the one who guides and leads. He protects and defends. And He is with you in it all.

This life is a big deal and your life really matters. Life is not about comfort, but it is about joy. By God's grace, make good decisions. Think about your decisions and remember, every step you take has meaning. Even the times you feel like you're going backwards, that is preparation for what's coming next.

So take the next step and move forward. That is my invitation to you. Do it with your whole heart and be prepared for all the good that God has in store for you.

ABOUT THE AUTHOR

Virgil D. DeJongh has a passion for strong and ethical leadership in life and in business. Recognized by his peers as a seasoned leader, he describes himself as a farmer at heart who loves his family. Helping people grow in their life experiences and financial well-being is his passion. He believes we are all called by God to leadership in life and business. He further believes that leaders welcome accountability, good counsel, and the challenges to leave meaningful legacies to their families, communities, indeed the world. Following his honorable discharge as a Vietnam Veteran, Virgil was the owner of a sizable farm operation for 15 years. In 1986, he founded and established the DeJongh Financial Group and has been recognized as a "Visionary leader", a top performer and keynote speaker in the Financial Services industry. He and Lavonne are leaders in their church and community and celebrate the joy of their three married children and 16 grandchildren. For the past 32 years, Virgil has created Financial guidance to help protect their families and their businesses. On April 20th of 2020 Virgil started a new and exciting venture, DeJongh Publishing and Consulting where he helps families leave their legacy as well as provides mentorship and consultation as people navigate change and growth in their lives.